BOOK 1

FIVE-STAR ENSEMBLES

FOR DIGITAL KEYBOARD ORCHESTRA

DENNIS ALEXANDER

Piano students traditionally spend most of their time at the piano alone—whether they are practicing or performing in a festival, concert, or competition. Young musicians who participate in band or orchestra always enjoy making music with their peers! Consequently, what could be more fun or exciting for pianists than performing in a large ensemble as members of a digital keyboard orchestra? These arrangements from my *Five-Star Solos* collections provide young pianists with an opportunity to create exciting and entertaining performances with other players with a minimum amount of stress and preparation! Each arrangement has five or six separate parts, with each part having an assigned general MIDI sound. Depending on the keyboard instruments being used, the conductor may find that the exact name for each part may differ slightly from instrument to instrument. However, all keyboard instruments that possess general MIDI sounds should be able to support the parts indicated.

Realize that some brands might have certain instruments that sound more realistic if performed an octave higher or lower than written. In other words, conductors and performers simply need to "use their ears" and musical judgment to determine what works best for each piece.

Each arrangement is presented in score format. All of the arrangements have five or six parts, but parts can be doubled or tripled for larger ensemble groups. The more players, the better! Depending on the number of players and the types of sounds used for each part, the conductor may wish to have some parts played at a higher or lower volume so that the end result is well balanced and pleasing to the ears of the listeners. I have indicated places where a melody line or accompaniment pattern is more easily executed with two hands. Notes on treble staves are to be played with the RH, except for those marked with *LH*; notes on bass staves are to be played with the LH, except for those marked with *RH*. Fingering for the RH is placed above the staff; fingering for the LH is placed below the staff.

Have fun and enjoy these motivating and exciting pieces with your group of "Digital Keyboard Orchestra" members! I hope that these arrangements bring a renewed enthusiasm for making music together.

Dedicated to my friend and colleague Lori Frazer, Yamaha Corporation of America, Keyboard Division, who has always been there for me with supportive assistance and expert advice

Alfred Alfred Music
P.O. Box 10003
Van Nuys, CA 91410-0003
alfred.com

ISBN-10: 1-4706-4221-2
ISBN-13: 978-1-4706-4221-1

Cover Photos
© Shutterstock: nav (keys), Yulia Glam (star) • © GettyImages: a-r-t-i-s-t (pattern), tarasov_vl (sax), fotoedu (castanets), ARTYuSTUDIO (clarinet), worac (dulcimer), venusphoto (flute), YinYang (drum), perets (trumpet), pepifoto (violin)

VICTORY MARCH!

Dennis Alexander

* For added stability, the thumb can be used to brace finger 3. The player may alternate hands ad lib.

Country Jamboree!

Dennis Alexander

TRIBAL DANCE

Quickly

Dennis Alexander

Forever True

Dennis Alexander

14

Scottish Highlanders

Very quickly

Dennis Alexander

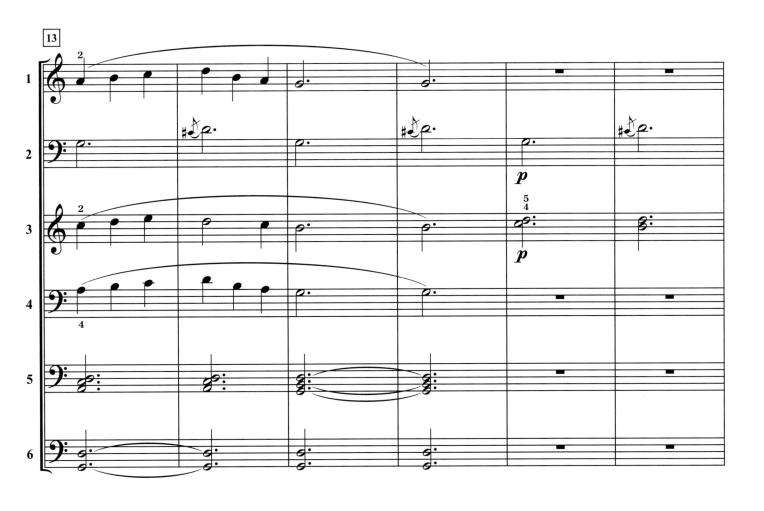

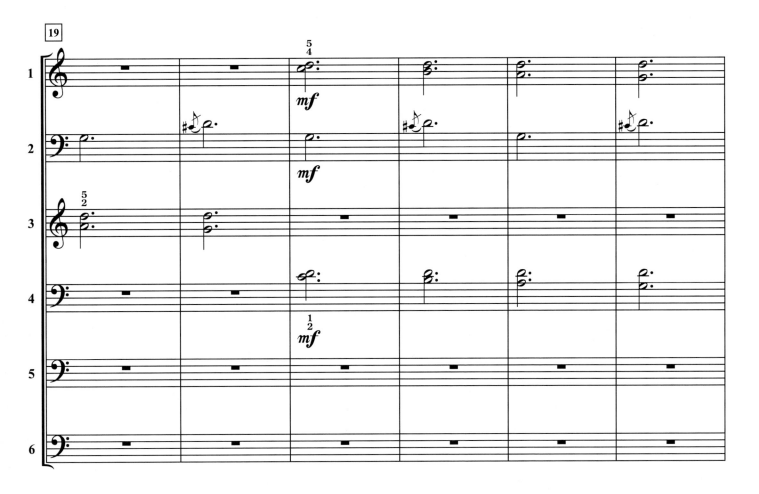

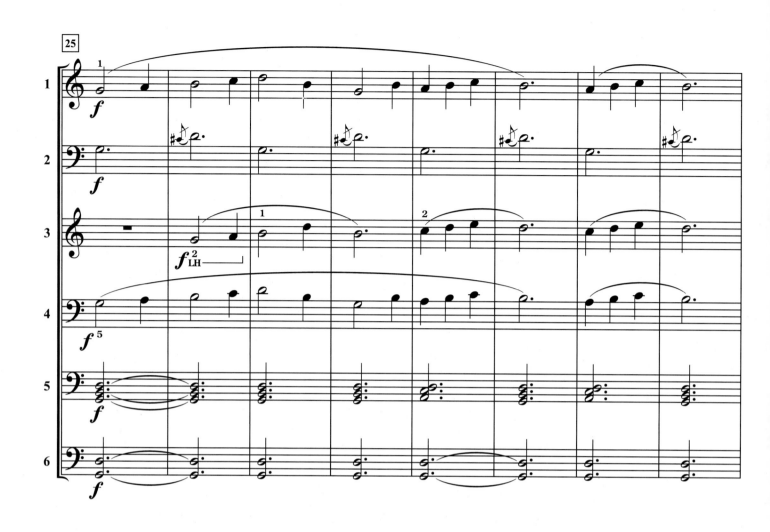

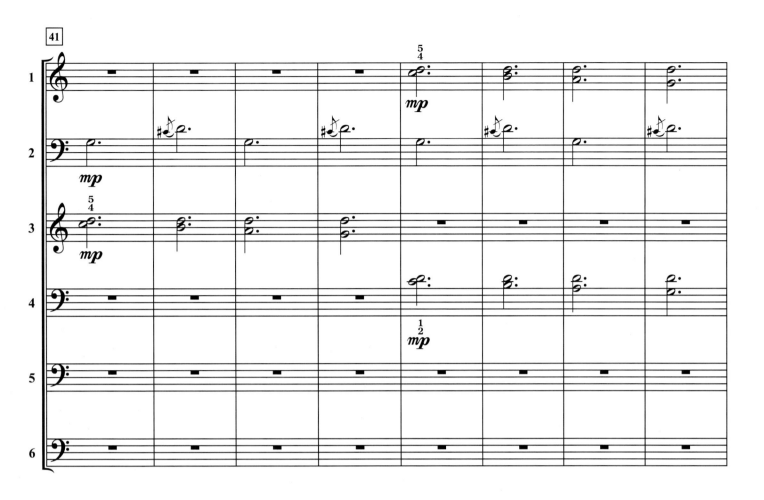

CRASH, BANG, BOOGIE!

Fast, and as loud as possible!

Dennis Alexander